Copyright © 2024 by CAMsDEN Publishing, LLC
ISBN: 978-1-963617-06-1

All rights reserved. No part of this publication may be reproduced, or transmitted in any form or by any means, including photocopying, recording, or other electronic or mechanical methods, without the prior written permission of the publisher.

Published by: CAMsDEN Publishing, LLC
Printed in the United States of America

Dear Parents,

Welcome to "Little Voices, Big Prayers!"—a place where the tender voices of our young ones rise in heartfelt prayer. This book is not just a collection of words; it's a starting point for a lifelong journey of faith and conversation with God.

As you share these pages with your child, you embark on a beautiful journey to instill the habit of prayer, making it as natural and essential as the loving exchanges that fill your days. "Little Voices, Big Prayers!" is designed to introduce children to the power of prayer, helping them understand how to pray, why we pray, and the significance of prayer in our daily lives.

Through simple, rhyming prayers tailored for morning, day, and night, this book aims to teach your child to reach out to God in every situation—from expressing joy and gratitude to seeking help and comfort. It's a way to guide them through their early steps in faith, laying a foundation that will support a growing, thriving spiritual life.

We hope that these prayers become a cornerstone for your child, helping them to voice their thoughts and feelings to God and understand that their words, however small, matter deeply. Thank you for allowing "Little Voices, Big Prayers!" to be a part of your child's spiritual growth. May it inspire them to build a lifelong relationship with God, filled with faith, hope, and love.

With heartfelt prayers and warmest wishes,

Leslie

The 3 P's of Prayer

Praying is like talking to God, and you can remember what to say with the 3 P's: Praise, Pardon, and Petition!

1. Praise (Say Nice Things about God)
Start by telling God what you love about Him. It's like giving a big thank you for all the good things!

Example: "God, You are great! Thanks for my family and the sunny days."

2. Pardon (Ask God to Forgive You/Say Sorry)
Next, tell God if you're sorry for something you did. He's always ready to forgive you.

Example: "Sorry, God, for not sharing my toys today. Please forgive me."

3. Petition (Ask God for Help or Something You Need)
Last, ask God for what you need, whether it's help, or something you're worried about.

Example: "Please help me do well in my game tomorrow, and keep my family safe."

Remember, God loves hearing from you at anytime, just like a best friend!

_____

Gratitude for a New Day

Thank You, God, for this lovely day.
For the sun that shines, and games we play.
Help us to laugh, to live, to love,
and feel Your warmth from up above.
In Jesus' name, Amen.

Psalm 5:3

Prayer Before Meals

Thank You God for our food so sweet;
the fruits, the veggies, the meats, the treats!
Bless the hands that made our meal.
Help us grow strong, with zeal.
In Jesus' name, Amen.

3 John 1:2

Prayer for Peace

Let peace dwell in our home, as you dwell near;
calm our worries, calm our fear.
May our words be soft, our hugs extra tight,
in our home, God, be our guiding light.
In Jesus' name, Amen.

John 14:27

Blessing for the Day Ahead

Guide our steps as we walk in Your light.
Keep us safe, hold our hands tight.
Help us to smile, to share, to care,
in every moment, here and there.
In Jesus' name, Amen.

Psalm 118:24

Prayer for Patience

When I'm hurried, or things aren't nice,
remind me, God, not being patience comes
with a price.
Help me to wait, help me to see,
patience brings good things to me.
In Jesus' name, Amen.

Romans 12:12

Prayer for Tomorrow

Prepare us for another day,
to walk in Your most perfect way.
Whatever comes, let us be ready,
as you have called us to be, strong and steady.
In Jesus' name, Amen.

Jeremiah 29:11

Prayer for Self-Love

Lord, help me to see myself as You see me;
beautiful and loved.
Let me walk with confidence, knowing I am
Your creation, wonderfully made.
In Jesus' name, Amen.

Psalm 139:14

Prayer for Forgiveness

For the wrongs we may have done today,
forgive us, God, this we pray.
Teach us to forgive just the same,
in Your holy and mighty name.
In Jesus' name, Amen.

Ephesians 4:32

Prayer for School

Bless me, God, as I learn and grow.
in my school where the knowledge flows.
Protect my friends and all we greet,
to spread God's love on repeat.
In Jesus' name, Amen.

Proverbs 1:5

Prayer for Honesty

God keep me honest, keep me clear.
Send Your truth for me to hear.
In my words and let my actions show,
that honesty is the best way to grow.
In Jesus' name, Amen.

Proverbs 12:22

Prayer for Future Aspirations

Lord, inspire my dreams so bright,
Guide my steps in Your holy light.
Show me the path I should take,
With passion and perseverance for Your sake.
In Jesus' name, Amen.

Proverbs 16:3

Prayer for Understanding

God help us to listen, help us to learn,
to understand each twist and turn.
In our talks and our plays,
let us find understanding ways.
In Jesus' name, Amen.

Proverbs 4:7

Prayer for Confidence

God help me face each fear and test,
with your courage, I am blessed.
I know through You, I can achieve,
all things great that I believe.
In Jesus' name, Amen.

Philippians 4:13

Courage for Challenges

When things get tough, and I'm feeling small,
remind me, God, that I can stand tall.
Give me courage at my call,
to face my fears, both big or small.
In Jesus' name, Amen.

Deuteronomy 31:6

Prayer for Friendship

God help me find friends, both loyal and true,
and be a good friend in all that I do.
Together we laugh, together we play,
God, make our friendships last day by day.
In Jesus' name, Amen.

Ecclesiastes 4:9-10

Prayer for Wisdom

God grant us wisdom, on this day.
In our choices and in our play.
Let us learn from mistakes we've made,
for in you wisdom, we have prayed.
In Jesus' name, Amen.

James 1:5

Prayer for Protection

Lord, watch over me on this day,
In all I do, in all I say.
Help me make decisions right,
keep me safe in Your sight.
In Jesus' name, Amen.

Psalm 121:7-8

Prayer for Love

God let love fill our hearts and our homes,
through hugs and kisses, make our love known.
May we love as we have been taught
loving our neighbor without a second thought.
In Jesus' name, Amen.

1 Corinthians 13:4-7

Prayer for Family

God bless my family every day,
keep them safe as they work and play.
Help us to cherish, love, and dream,
following Your guide, working together
as a team.
In Jesus' name, Amen.

Proverbs 17:17

Prayer for Compassion

God teach me kindness and teach me to care;
to see someone in need and to be there.
To share a smile or to lend a hand,
to spread Your love across the land.
In Jesus' name, Amen.

Colossians 3:12

Prayer for Strength

God give us strength to face each task,
reading Your word, preparing to ask.
When we're weak, make us strong,
in Your arms, where we belong.
In Jesus' name, Amen.

Isaiah 41:10

Prayer for Humility

God teach us humility and to see,
we need Your help, to be set free.
Let us ask when we don't know,
and in Your grace, let us grow.
In Jesus' name, Amen.

Philippians 2:3-4

Prayer for Gratitude

Dear God, as I end my day,
I thank You for Your loving way.
Help me rest well through the night,
under Your watchful, loving sight.
In Jesus' name, Amen.

Psalm 4:7-8

Prayer for Restful Sleep

Now it's time to rest our heads,
sleep in peace in our beds.
God watch over us through the night,
till morning comes with new light.
In Jesus' name, Amen.

Psalm 121:3-4

Dear little prayer warriors,

Remember, talking to God is something you can do every day, no matter what you're feeling or facing. Whether you're joyful, worried, thankful, or in need of a friend, God is always listening.

Make prayer a part of your daily adventure, and see how it fills your life with peace and strength.

Happy Praying and God Bless!

We'd love to hear about your prayer journeys and see how you're growing in faith.

Scan QR Code to connect with us on Instagram to share your stories, get encouragement, and be part of our praying community.

Check out more of our books: www.LeslieNClark.com

www.ingramcontent.com/pod-product-compliance
Lightning Source LLC
Chambersburg PA
CBHW061350010526
44107CB00011B/889